The
Book of
POWER WORDS

AFFIRMATIONS/ CUT OUTS FOR VISION BOARD AND JOURNALS

What a great way to begin on your vision boards and start to manifest the life you desire! Inside are colorful cutouts, motivational quotes you can frame and hang, blank checks to write to yourself, lined and blank pages and much more.

You can use this book as your personal "vision board book" or journal. Start living the life you visualize and desire.

"*Words have energy and power with the ability to help, to heal, to hinder, to hurt, to harm, to humiliate and to humble.*"

-Yehuda Berg

SPEAK TO YOURSELF KINDLY

The book of power words

The book of power words

The book of power words.

You are in control of your own reality and It starts with you, NOW!

This book of power words and affirmations is designed to help you visualize and create of a life you deserve and to help you remain positive and grateful while manifesting. This can be cut out and placed anywhere or used for your journal or vision board.

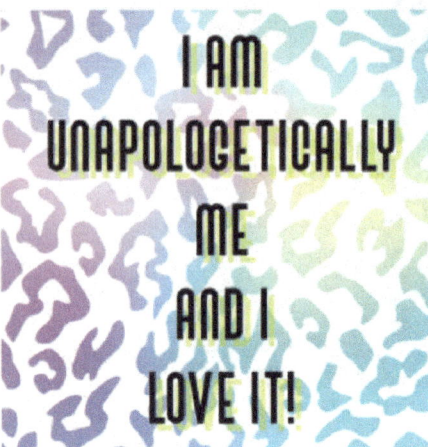

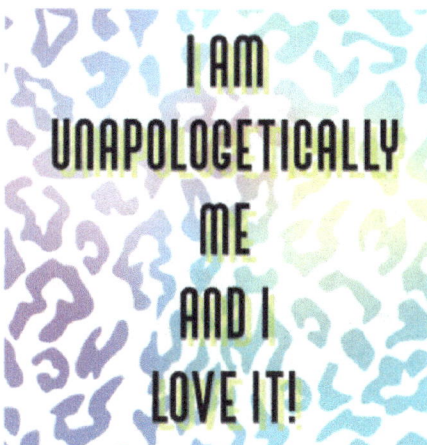

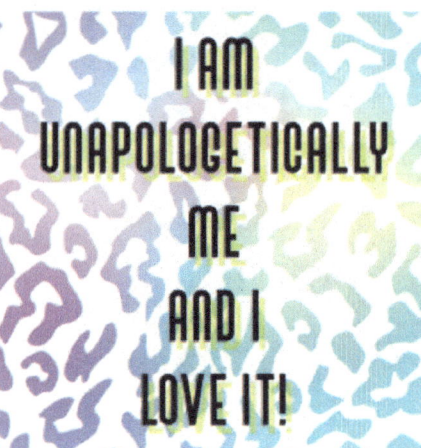

IMAGINATION IS GREATER THAN INTELLIGENCE, THERE'S NO LIMITS!

The book of power words

I AM ABUNDANT

I AM PROSPEROUS

I AM GRATEFUL

I AM CONSISTENT
I AM THE ONLY PERSON WHO CAN STOP ME

Co-Author of my Story

be grateful

I CREATE MY FUTURE NOW

Life doesn't just happen, I make it happen

I get things done now.

Everything I tough turns to gold!

THINGS ALWAYS WORKS OUT FOR ME IN THE END.

The book of power words

Good Vibes Only

Good Vibes Only

The book of power words

Only YOU can stop YOU!

The book of power words

I am always at the RIGHT place at the RIGHT time.

— MARK HAUGHTON

SPEAK TO
YOURSELF
KINDLY

The book of power words

2815

Date _____

Pay to the
Order of _____ $ [   ]

_____ Dollars

Memo _____

:18571   :1863887571   11638;

2815

Date _____

Pay to the
Order of _____ $ [   ]

_____ Dollars

Memo _____

:18571   :1863887571   11638;

2815

Date _____

Pay to the
Order of _____ $ [   ]

_____ Dollars

Memo _____

:18571   :1863887571   11638;

	2815
	Date _____

Pay to the
Order of _____ $ [____]

_____ Dollars

Memo _____ _____

:18571 :1863887571 11638;

	2815
	Date _____

Pay to the
Order of _____ $ [____]

_____ Dollars

Memo _____ _____

:18571 :1863887571 11638;

	2815
	Date _____

Pay to the
Order of _____ $ [____]

_____ Dollars

Memo _____ _____

:18571 :1863887571 11638;

	2815
	Date _____

Pay to the
Order of _____ $ [_____]

_____ Dollars

Memo _____ _____

:18571   :1863887571   11638;

	2815
	Date _____

Pay to the
Order of _____ $ [_____]

_____ Dollars

Memo _____ _____

:18571   :1863887571   11638;

	2815
	Date _____

Pay to the
Order of _____ $ [_____]

_____ Dollars

Memo _____ _____

:18571   :1863887571   11638;

	2815
	Date _____
Pay to the Order of _____	$ [____]
_____ Dollars	
Memo _____ _____	
:18571 :1863887571 11638;	

	2815
	Date _____
Pay to the Order of _____	$ [____]
_____ Dollars	
Memo _____ _____	
:18571 :1863887571 11638;	

	2815
	Date _____
Pay to the Order of _____	$ [____]
_____ Dollars	
Memo _____ _____	
:18571 :1863887571 11638;	

	2815
	Date _____
Pay to the Order of _____	$ [_____]
_____ Dollars
Memo _____ _____
:18571   :1863887571   11638;

	2815
	Date _____
Pay to the Order of _____	$ [_____]
_____ Dollars
Memo _____ _____
:18571   :1863887571   11638;

	2815
	Date _____
Pay to the Order of _____	$ [_____]
_____ Dollars
Memo _____ _____
:18571   :1863887571   11638;

Check 1

2815

Date _____

Pay to the Order of _____ $ [_____]

_____ Dollars

Universal Bank Of Belief
777 Planet Earth
Manifest the Life You Desire

Memo _____   _____

:18571   :1863887571   11638;

Watermark: Money comes to me

Check 2

2815

Date _____

Pay to the Order of _____ $ [_____]

_____ Dollars

Universal Bank Of Belief
777 Planet Earth
Manifest the Life You Desire

Memo _____   _____

:18571   :1863887571   11638;

Watermark: I Am Worthy

Check 3

2815

Date _____

Pay to the Order of _____ $ [_____]

_____ Dollars

Universal Bank Of Belief
777 Planet Earth
Manifest the Life You Desire

Memo _____   _____

:18571   :1863887571   11638;

Watermark: Money comes to me Effortlessly

Check 1

2815

Date _____

Pay to the Order of _____ $ _____

_____ Dollars

I Deserve the Best

Universal Bank Of Belief
777 Planet Earth
Manifest the Life You Desire

Memo _____

:18571   :1863887571   11638;

Check 2

2815

Date _____

Pay to the Order of _____ $ _____

_____ Dollars

I Am Worthy

Universal Bank Of Belief
777 Planet Earth
Manifest the Life You Desire

Memo _____

:18571   :1863887571   11638;

Check 3

2815

Date _____

Pay to the Order of _____ $ _____

_____ Dollars

Money comes to me Effortlessly

Universal Bank Of Belief
777 Planet Earth
Manifest the Life You Desire

Memo _____

:18571   :1863887571   11638;

	2815
	Date _____

Pay to the
Order of _____ $ [ ]
_____ Dollars

Universal Bank Of Belief
777 Planet Earth
Manifest the Life You Desire

Memo _____ _____
:18571   :1863887571   11638;

Money comes to me

	2815
	Date _____

Pay to the
Order of _____ $ [ ]
_____ Dollars

Universal Bank Of Belief
777 Planet Earth
Manifest the Life You Desire

Memo _____ _____
:18571   :1863887571   11638;

I Am Worthy

	2815
	Date _____

Pay to the
Order of _____ $ [ ]
_____ Dollars

Universal Bank Of Belief
777 Planet Earth
Manifest the Life You Desire

Memo _____ _____
:18571   :1863887571   11638;

Money comes to me Effortlessly

Check 1 (navy border)

2815

Date _____

Pay to the Order of _____ $ _____

_____ Dollars

Universal Bank Of Belief
777 Planet Earth
Manifest the Life You Desire

Memo _____

⑈18571   ⑈1863887571   11638⑈

Watermark: I Deserve the Best

Check 2 (light blue border)

2815

Date _____

Pay to the Order of _____ $ _____

_____ Dollars

Universal Bank Of Belief
777 Planet Earth
Manifest the Life You Desire

Memo _____

⑈18571   ⑈1863887571   11638⑈

Watermark: I Am Worthy

Check 3 (purple border)

2815

Date _____

Pay to the Order of _____ $ _____

_____ Dollars

Universal Bank Of Belief
777 Planet Earth
Manifest the Life You Desire

Memo _____

⑈18571   ⑈1863887571   11638⑈

Watermark: Money comes to me Effortlessly

Check 1

2815

Date _____

Pay to the Order of _____ $ [ ]

_____ Dollars

Universal Bank Of Belief
777 Planet Earth
Manifest the Life You Desire

Memo _____

:18571   :1863887571   11638;

Watermark: Money comes to me

Check 2

2815

Date _____

Pay to the Order of _____ $ [ ]

_____ Dollars

Universal Bank Of Belief
777 Planet Earth
Manifest the Life You Desire

Memo _____

:18571   :1863887571   11638;

Watermark: I Am Worthy

Check 3

2815

Date _____

Pay to the Order of _____ $ [ ]

_____ Dollars

Universal Bank Of Belief
777 Planet Earth
Manifest the Life You Desire

Memo _____

:18571   :1863887571   11638;

Watermark: Money comes to me Effortlessly

MAKE MONEY

PROFIT

Fear
less

THOUGHTS BECOMES WORDS...

The book of power words.

I am amazing

I am abundant

I am beautiful

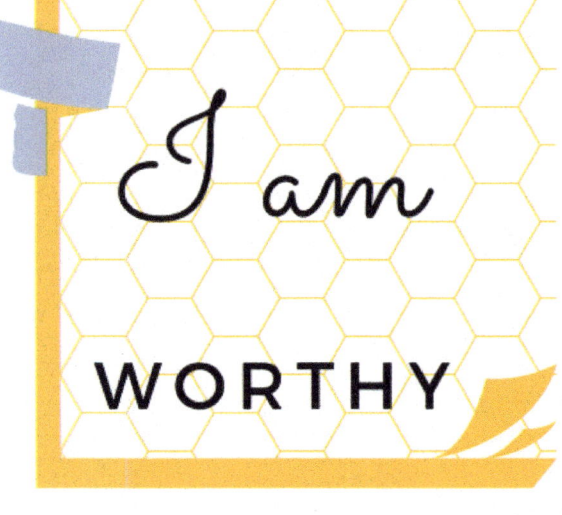

I am WORTHY

Stay Fearless

So Proud of
YOU

GREAT THINGS ALWAYS HAPPENS FOR ME

I AM ALWAYS WINNING

I WAS BORN TO BE ABUNDANT

I always have good opportunities available to me

I AM ALWAYS AT THE RIGHT PLACE AT THE RIGHT TIME.

I always share my abundance openly

Life is full of potential to Create wealth and abundance

The book of power words

BE BRAVE

I have more than enough

The book of power words

I AM HAPPY

I deserve the best

I am great

You're unstoppable When you really want it

I Will Get Things accomplished

I REFUSE TO GIVE UP

THINK POSITIVE

I have so much confidence

I'M GOING TO MAKE YOU SO PROUD.
- note to self.

My presence Is power

Love

I ACCEPT ONLY THE BEST

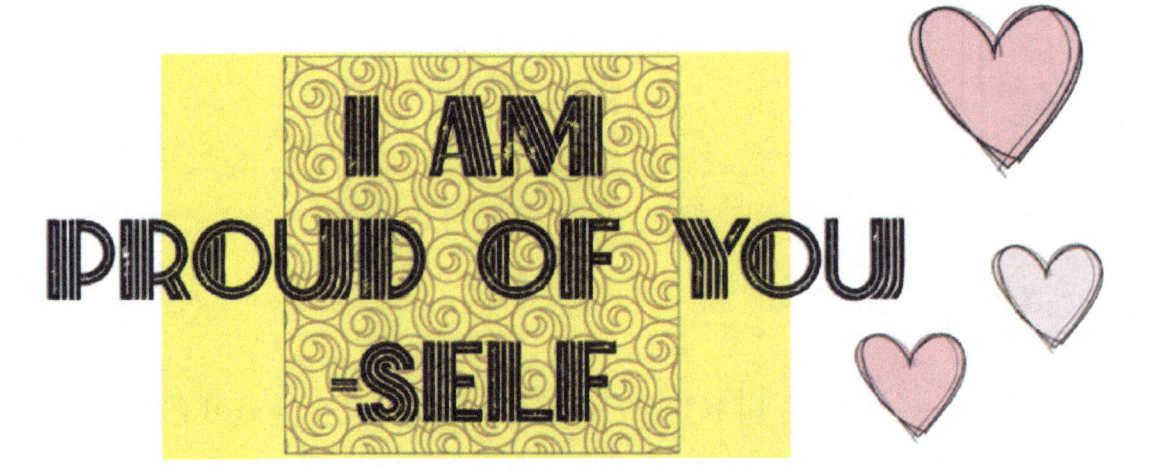

KEEP GOING

I AM PROUD OF YOU
-SELF

THOUGHTS
BECOMES
WORDS...

The book of power words.

I love to feel inspired

I believe in the person I dream of becoming

i love my body

I am at peace with who I am

Now I am creating my life exactly how I want it.

I ACCEPT MYSELF UNCONDITIONALLY

I love My Life

I honor my commitments To Myself

i love to inspire others

I choose to be happy and courageously love myself today

I LOVE TO LAUGH

I LOVE MY HOME

I AM FREE OF WORRY

I LOVE THE SKIN I AM IN

I ATTRACT PEOPLE WHO LOVES ME

I attract people who respects me

The book of power words

I AM A SURVIVOR

I AM WORTHY

I forgive the young me

@THEBOOKOFPOWERWORDS777

I AM STRONG

I AM AN OVERCOMER

I AM FIERCE

I AM HEALTHY

I AM HEALED

I'M DOPE ASF

I am who I say I am

I AM DESERVING

You are awesome

I AM A MAGNET OF ALL THINGS GOOD

The book of power words

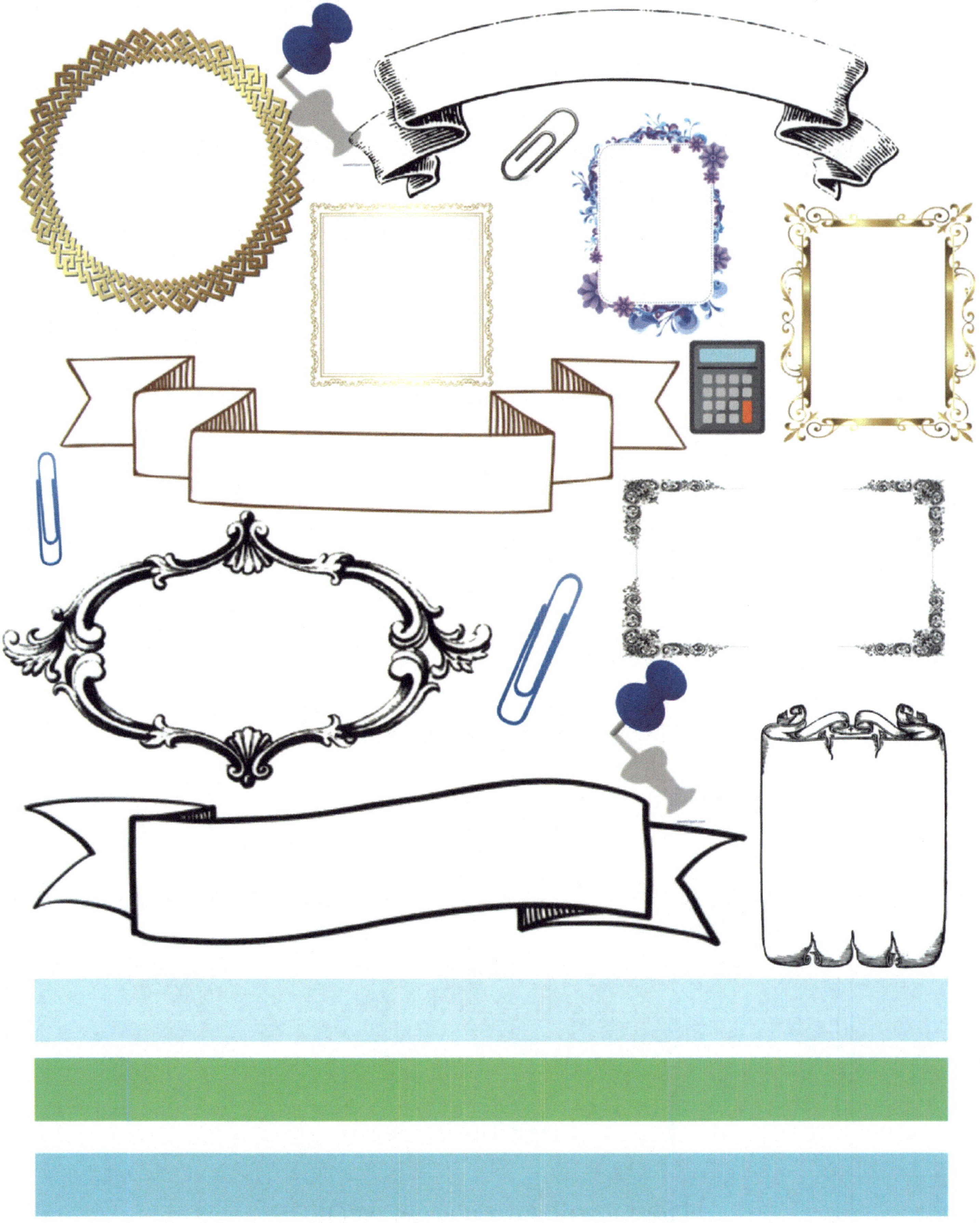

SPEAK TO YOURSELF KINDLY

The book of power words

BOSS BOSS BOSS
BOSS BOSS BOSS
BOSS BOSS BOSS
BOSS BOSS BOSS
BOSS BOSS

The book of power words

Manifest That $HIT

THOUGHTS
BECOMES
WORDS...

The book of power words.

WALLET AFFIRMATION CARDS

Write down you affirmations and store in your wallet, and every time you reach into your wallet, read your affirmations

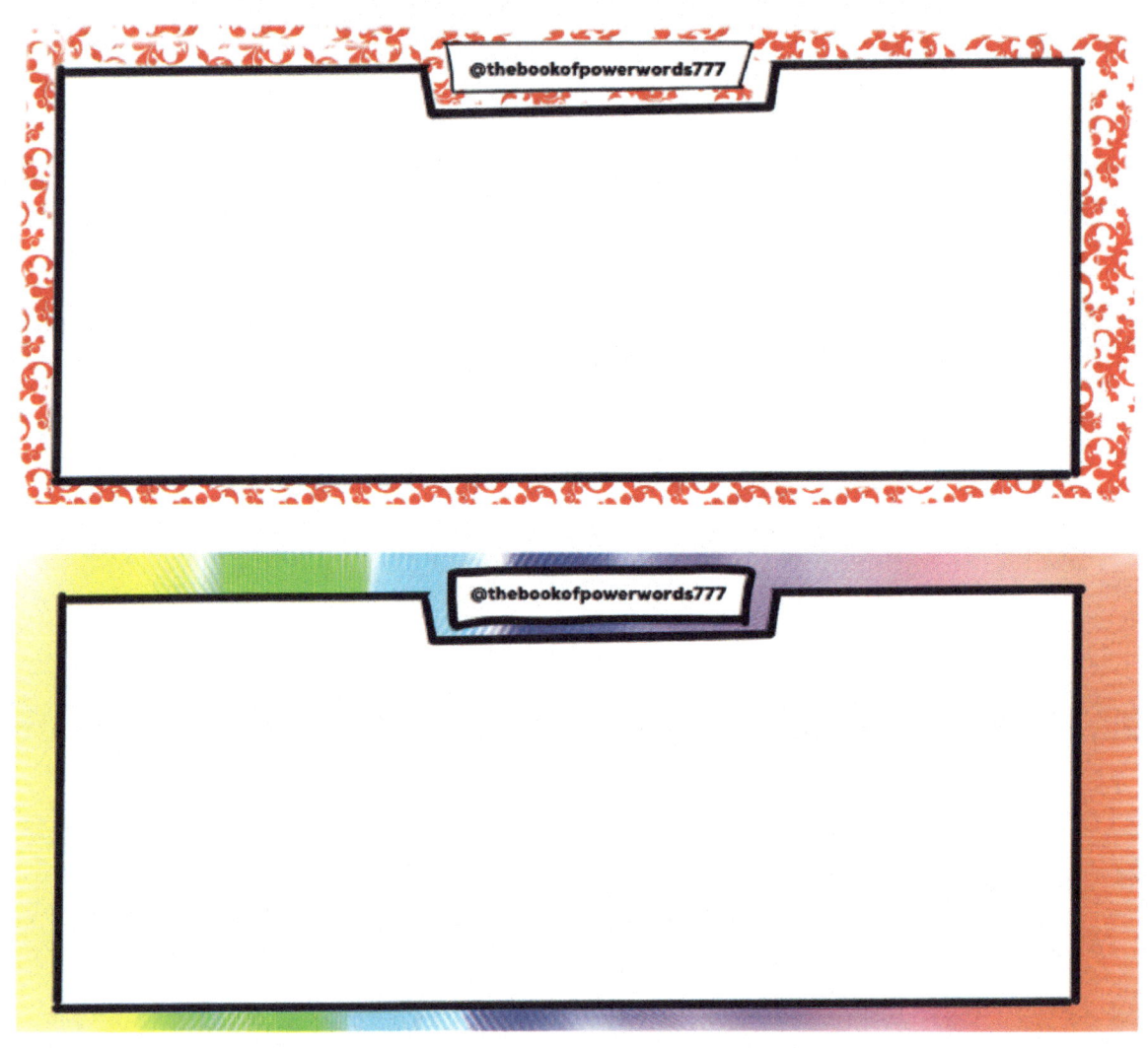

@thebookofpowerwords777

@thebookofpowerwords777

Affirm the monetary abundance you'd like to receive.

The Universal Bank of God
@thebookofpowerwords777

2815

Date _____

Pay to the
Order of _____ $ _____

_____ Dollars

Memo _____ _____

:18571   :1863887571   11638; *@thebookofpowerwords*

The book of power words

P.S. love you

SPEAK TO
YOURSELF
KINDLY

The book of power words

Hey beautiful!

THOUGHTS
BECOMES
WORDS...

The book of power words.

you Are so dope

Girl, you're so damn Beautiful!

HAVE A GREAT DAY!

BOY, U ARE HANDSOME

Pssst, HEY, yeah you, HELLO BEAU TI FUL!

The book of power words

BE
Positive

The book of power words

BE GREAT

THOUGHTS
BECOMES
WORDS...

The book of power words.

MAKE *Today* AMAZING

The book of power words

you are WORTHY

I AM GRATEFUL

SPEAK TO YOURSELF KINDLY

The book of power words

DESERVE THE BEST

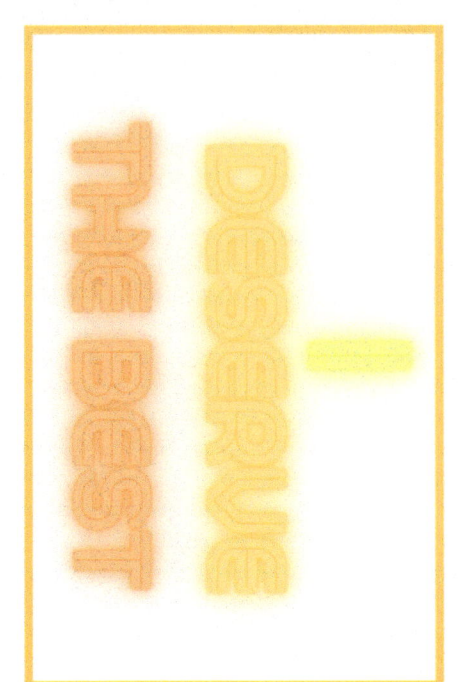

Shine

BOO!

EVERYTHING ALWAYS
WORKS OUT

THOUGHTS
BECOMES
WORDS.

The book of power words.

DO WHAT YOU LOVE ♡

The book of power words

DO WHAT YOU LOVE ♡

SPEAK TO YOURSELF KINDLY

The book of power words

DO WHAT YOU LOVE ♡

The book of power words

MY CONFIDENCE AND HAPPINESS INCREASE IN MY SLEEP

you deserve peace

YOU DESERVE HONESTY

I am aligning with all the wealth that awaits for me.

SPEAK TO YOURSELF KINDLY

The book of power words

WORK HARD REST OFTEN

THOUGHTS BECOMES WORDS...

The book of power words.

Time to think about SUCCESS

always at the right place at the right time

I am powerful and in control of my reality

OPPORTUNITIES Are Always Present

I attract all that is good

The book of power words

- Great things are always happening to me!
- I am limitless
- DOPE AF
- I appreciate the abundant opportunities tomorrow brings
- I am financially free
- I bet on me everytime

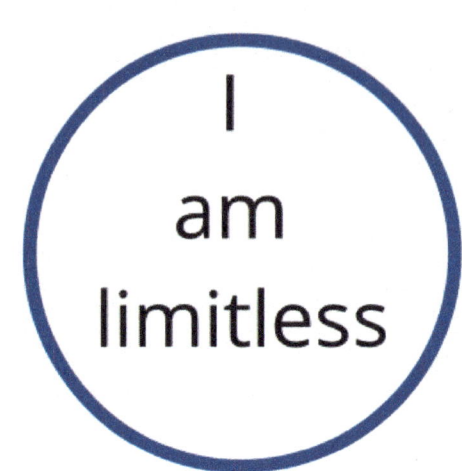

SPEAK TO YOURSELF KINDLY

The book of power words

Prove them
WRONG

The book of power words

I ADORE THE PERSON I SEE IN THE MIRROR

I light up every room that I walk into

Sucess

I attract everything I desire with ease

ANY AND EVERYTHING THAT I WANT, I ALWAYS GET.

I embody the highest version of myself

THOUGHTS BECOMES WORDS...

The book of power words.

SPEAK
IT
INTO
EXISTENCE,
Hunni.

The book of power words

ACTION

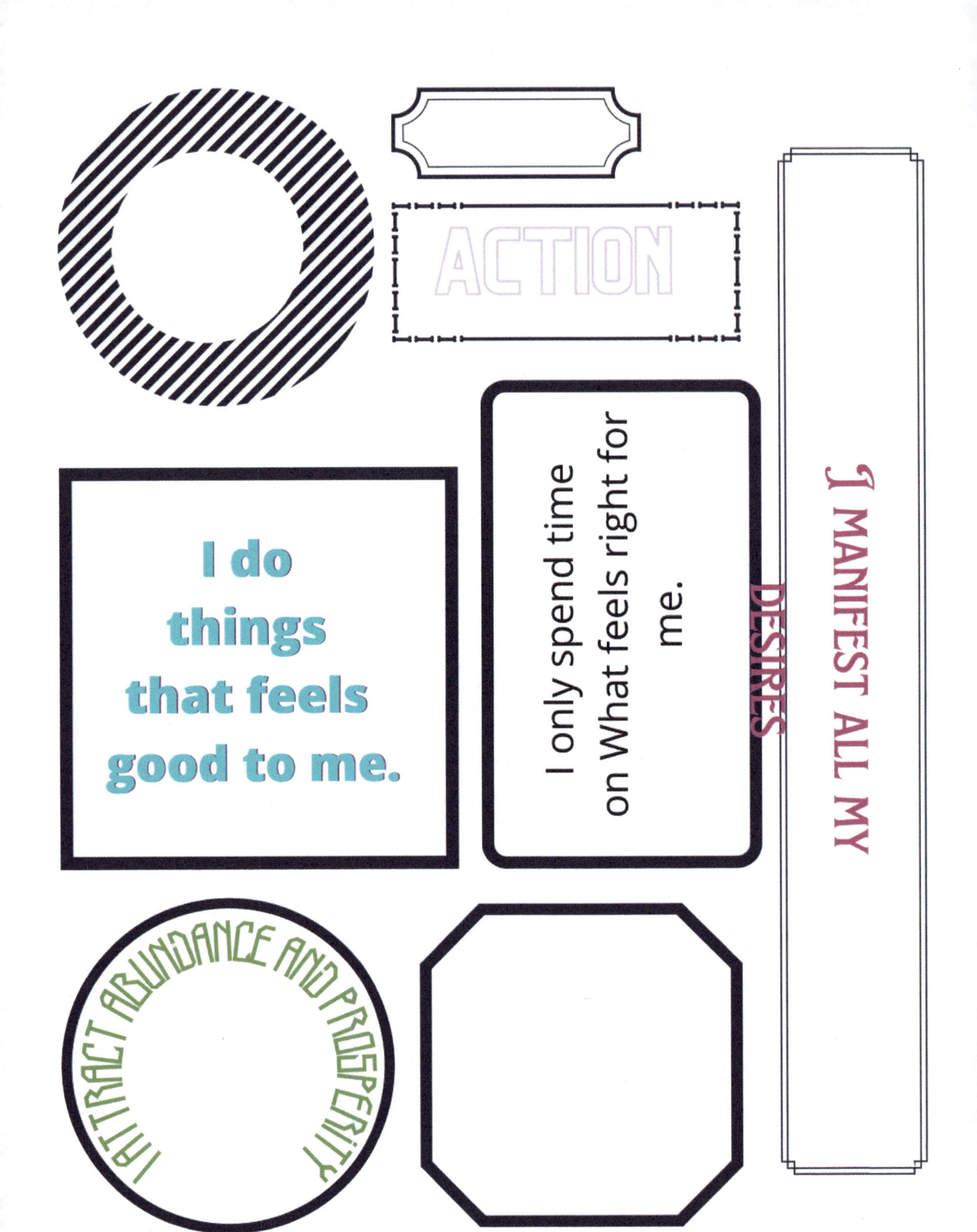

I do
things
that feels
good to me.

I only spend time
on What feels right for
me.

DESIRES

I MANIFEST ALL MY

I ATTRACT ABUNDANCE AND PROSPERITY

THOUGHTS
BECOMES
WORDS.

The book of power words.

Goals

Love surrounds me

I am entering the most successful year of my life

The book of power words

MY CREDIT SCORE _____

CREDIT SCORE

BILLS TO PAY OFF	BUDGET/CUT BACKS

THOUGHTS BECOMES WORDS...

The book of power words.

APPROVED

APPROVED

APPROVED

SPEAK TO
YOURSELF
KINDLY

The book of power words

©COOLHOUSECONCEPTS.COM

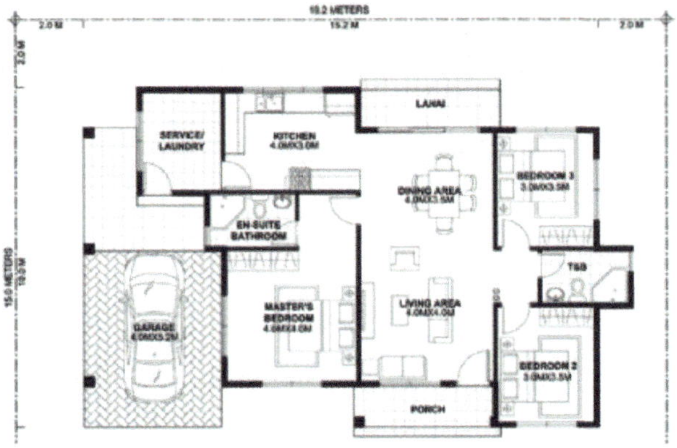
19.2 METERS
2.0 M
15.2 M
LANAI
SERVICE/ LAUNDRY
KITCHEN 4.0MX3.0M
DINING AREA 4.0MX3.5M
BEDROOM 3 3.0MX3.5M
EN-SUITE BATHROOM
T&B
MASTER'S BEDROOM 4.0MX4.0M
LIVING AREA 4.0MX4.0M
GARAGE 4.0MX5.2M
BEDROOM 2 3.0MX3.5M
PORCH

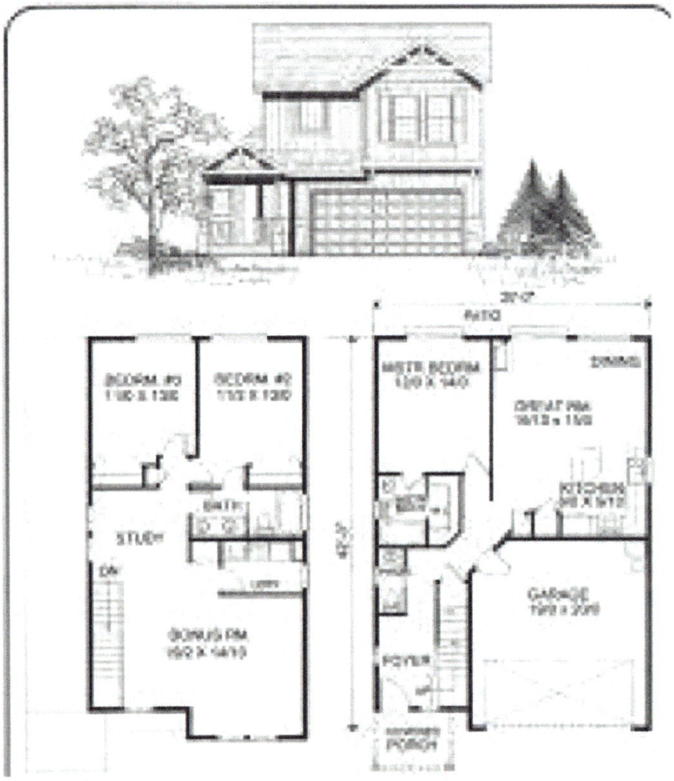
PATIO
BEDRM #3
BEDRM #2
BATH
STUDY
BONUS RM
MSTR BEDRM
GREAT RM
DINING
KITCHEN
GARAGE
FOYER
PORCH

©COOLHOUSECONCEPTS.COM

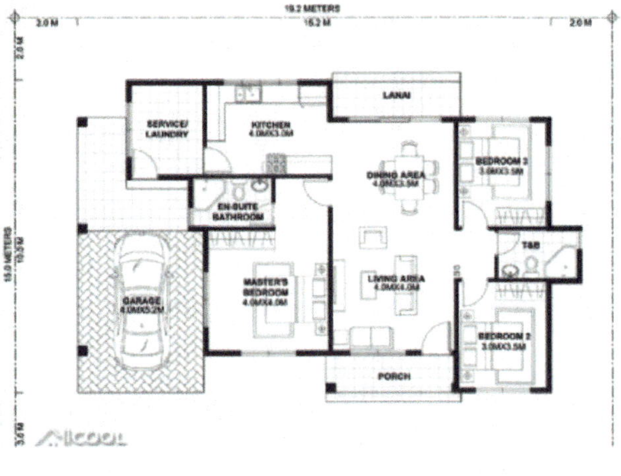
19.2 METERS
2.0 M
15.2 M
LANAI
SERVICE/ LAUNDRY
KITCHEN 4.0MX3.0M
DINING AREA 4.0MX3.5M
BEDROOM 3 3.0MX3.5M
EN-SUITE BATHROOM
T&B
MASTER'S BEDROOM 4.0MX4.0M
LIVING AREA 4.0MX4.0M
GARAGE 4.0MX5.2M
BEDROOM 2 3.0MX3.5M
PORCH

STUDY 13' x 14'
MSTR SUITE 20' x 21'
HIS
HERS
MSTR BATH
GYM 7' x 13'
BR 2 12' x 14'
LIVING 13' x 15'
VERANDA
PORCH
GRAND FOYER
MUSIC 10' x 11'
DINING 13' x 15'
BRKFST 12' x 14'
FAMILY 21' x 23'
GALLERY
2 CAR GARAGE 23' x 23'
1 CAR GARAGE 11' x 23'
UTIL
© ARCHIVAL DESIGNS, INC.

The book of power words

TICKET

TICKET

First Class

The book of power words.

Travel

Adventure Awaits

Money Moves

Journey

New day Fresh start

UNDER CONSTRUCTION!

WANDERLUST

I OVERCOME MY FEARS BY FOLLOWING MY DREAMS

SEE NEW HORIZONS

I AM ADVENTUROUS

THOUGHTS BECOMES WORDS...

The book of power words.

NORD.
N.Est.
E.N.Est.
EST.
E.S.Est.
S.Est.
S.S.Est.
SVD.
S.S.Ouest.
S.Ouest.
O.S.Ouest.
N.Ouest.
DEL
Antillas

THOUGHTS BECOMES WORDS...

The book of power words.

I woke up like this..
GRATEFUL

SPEAK TO YOURSELF KINDLY

The book of power words

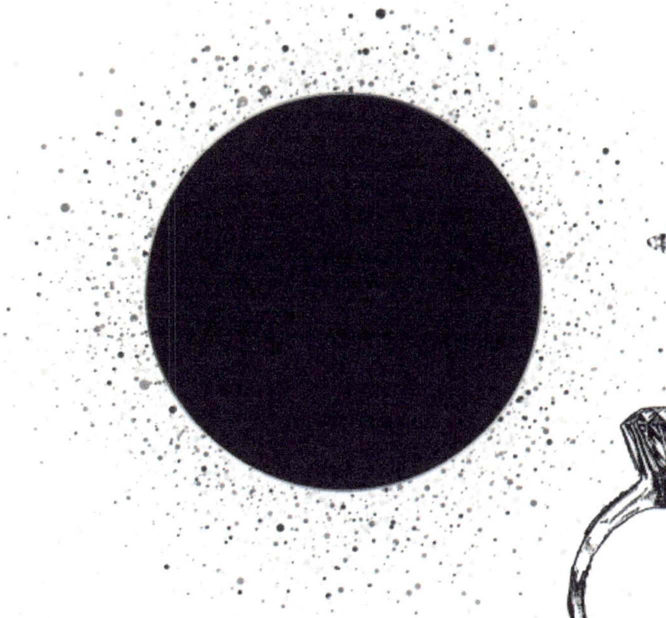
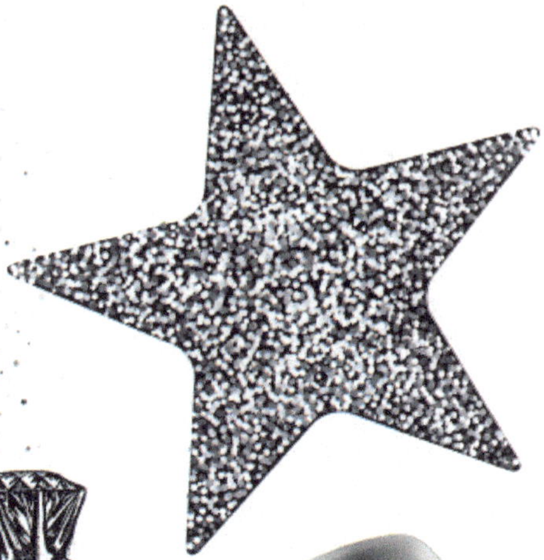
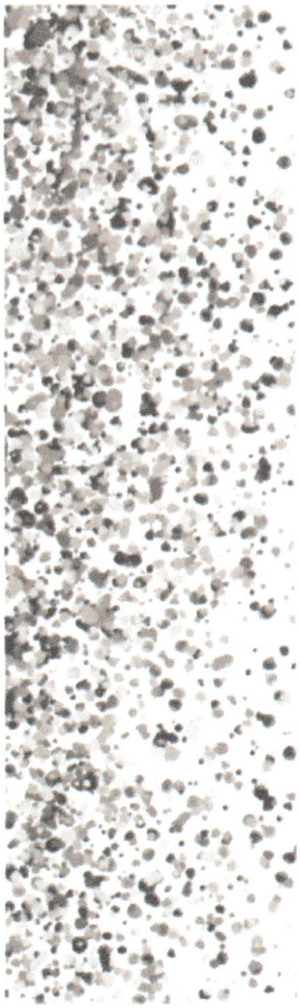
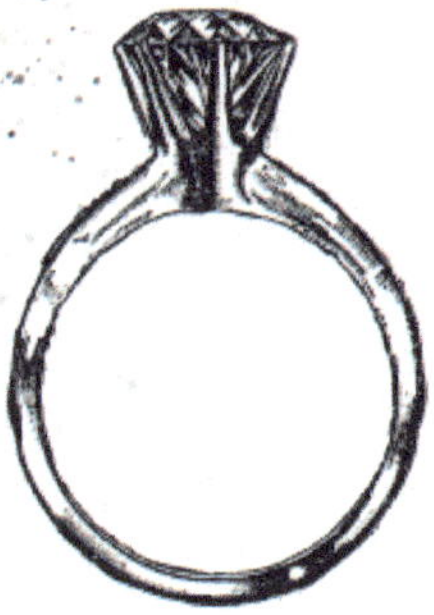
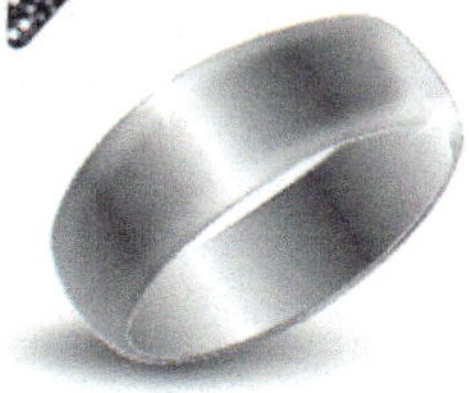
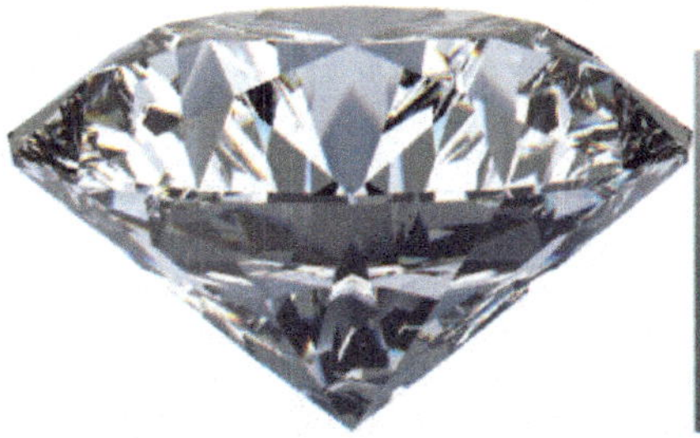

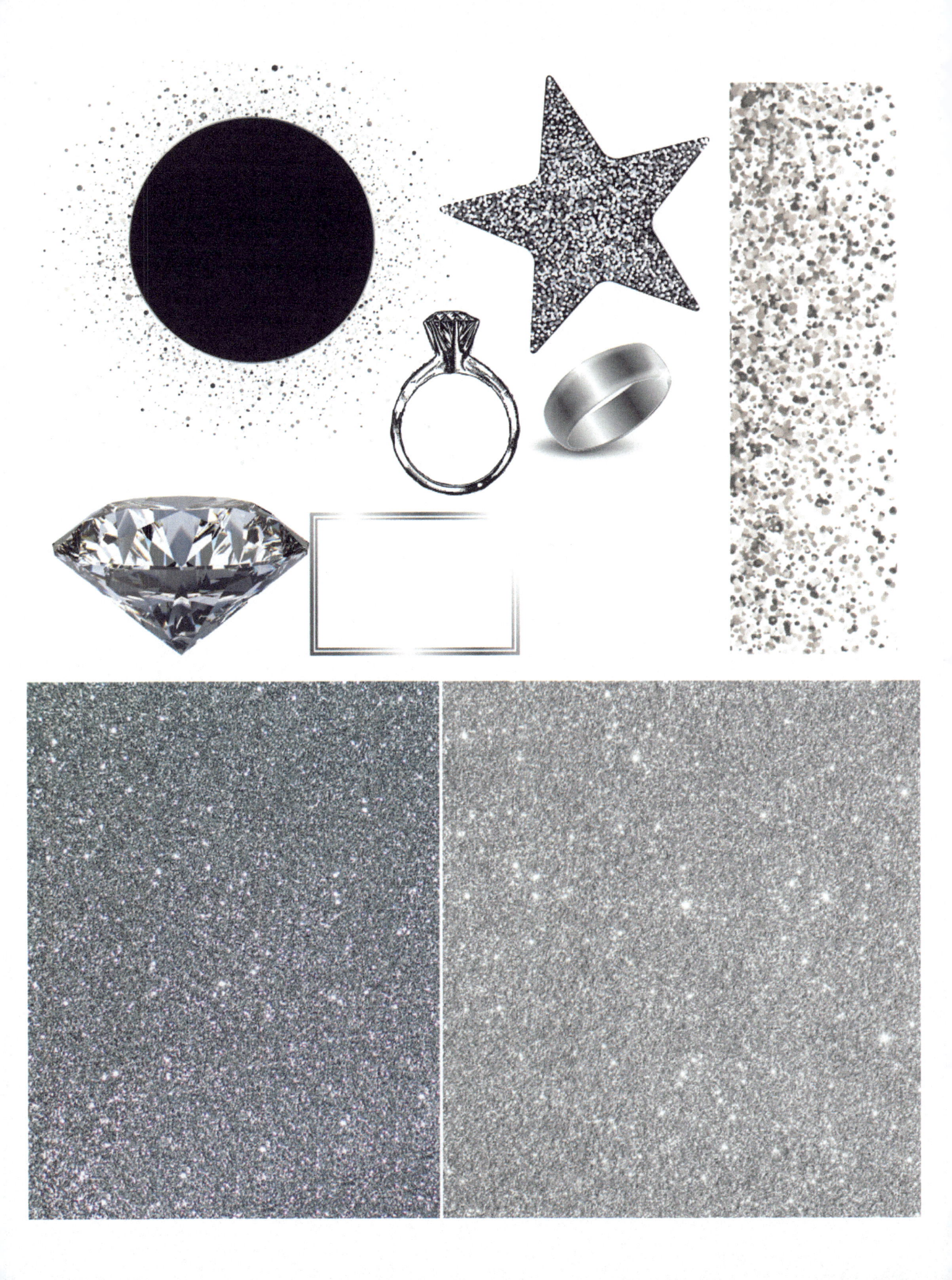

SPEAK TO YOURSELF KINDLY

The book of power words

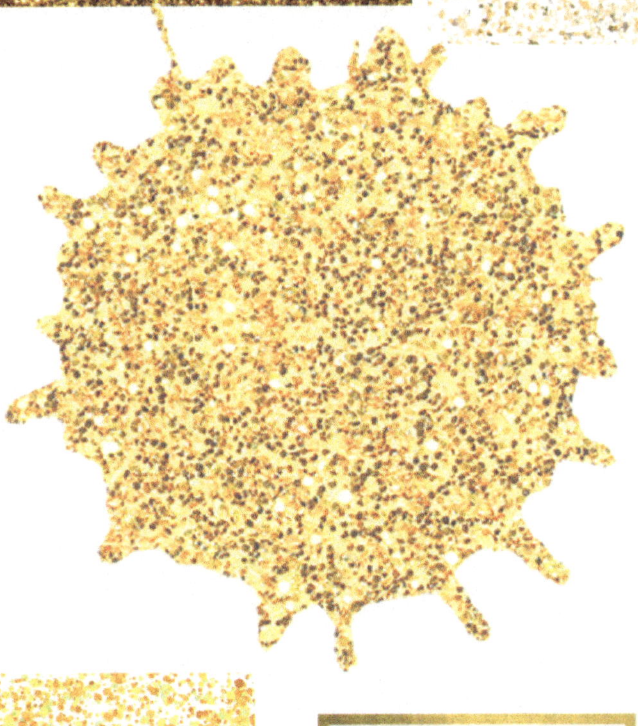
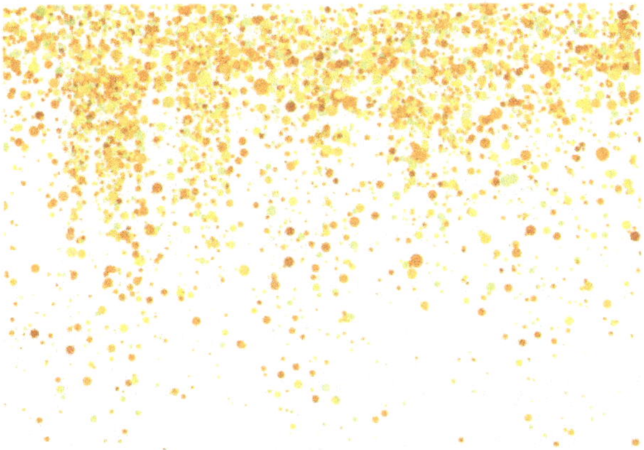

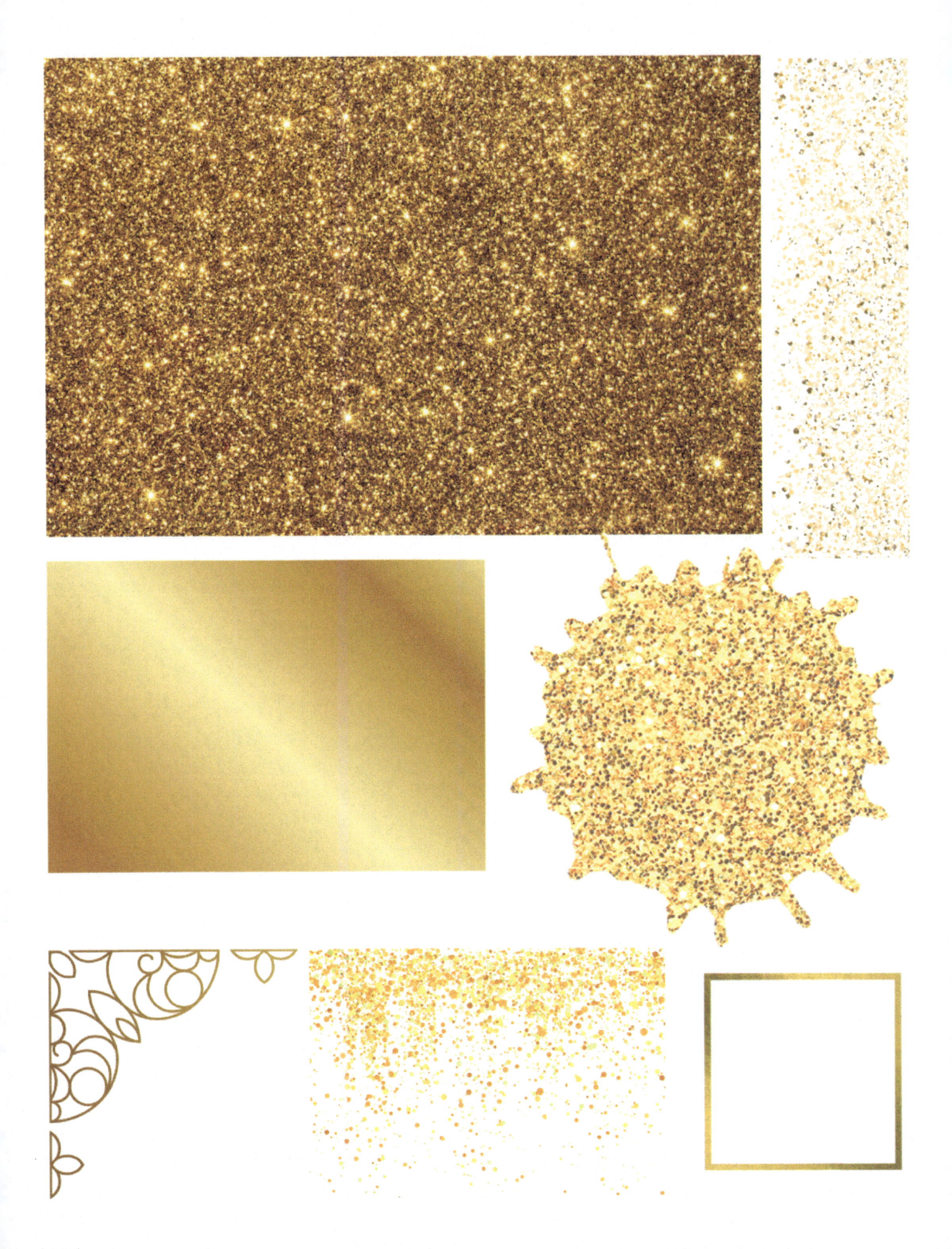

The book of power words

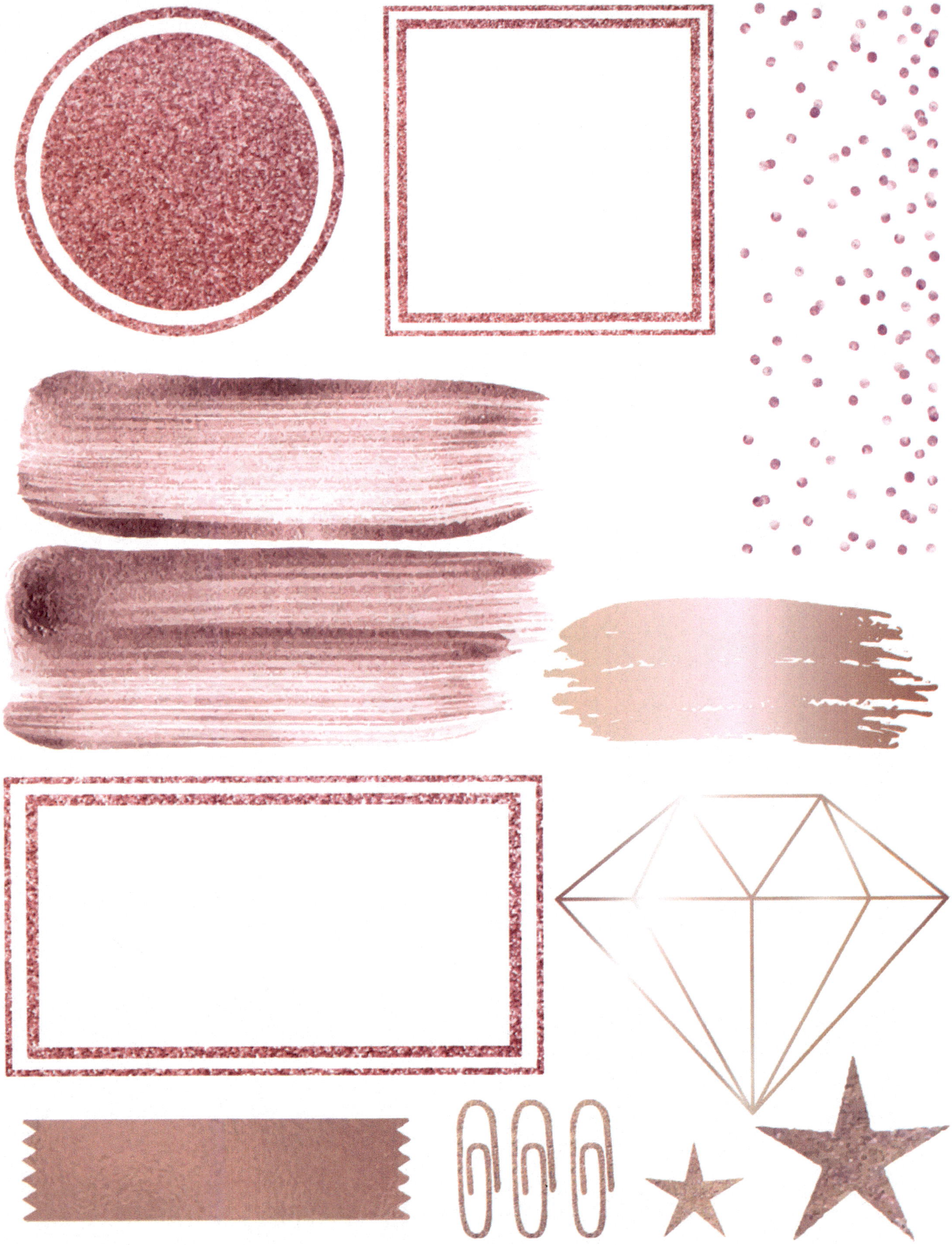

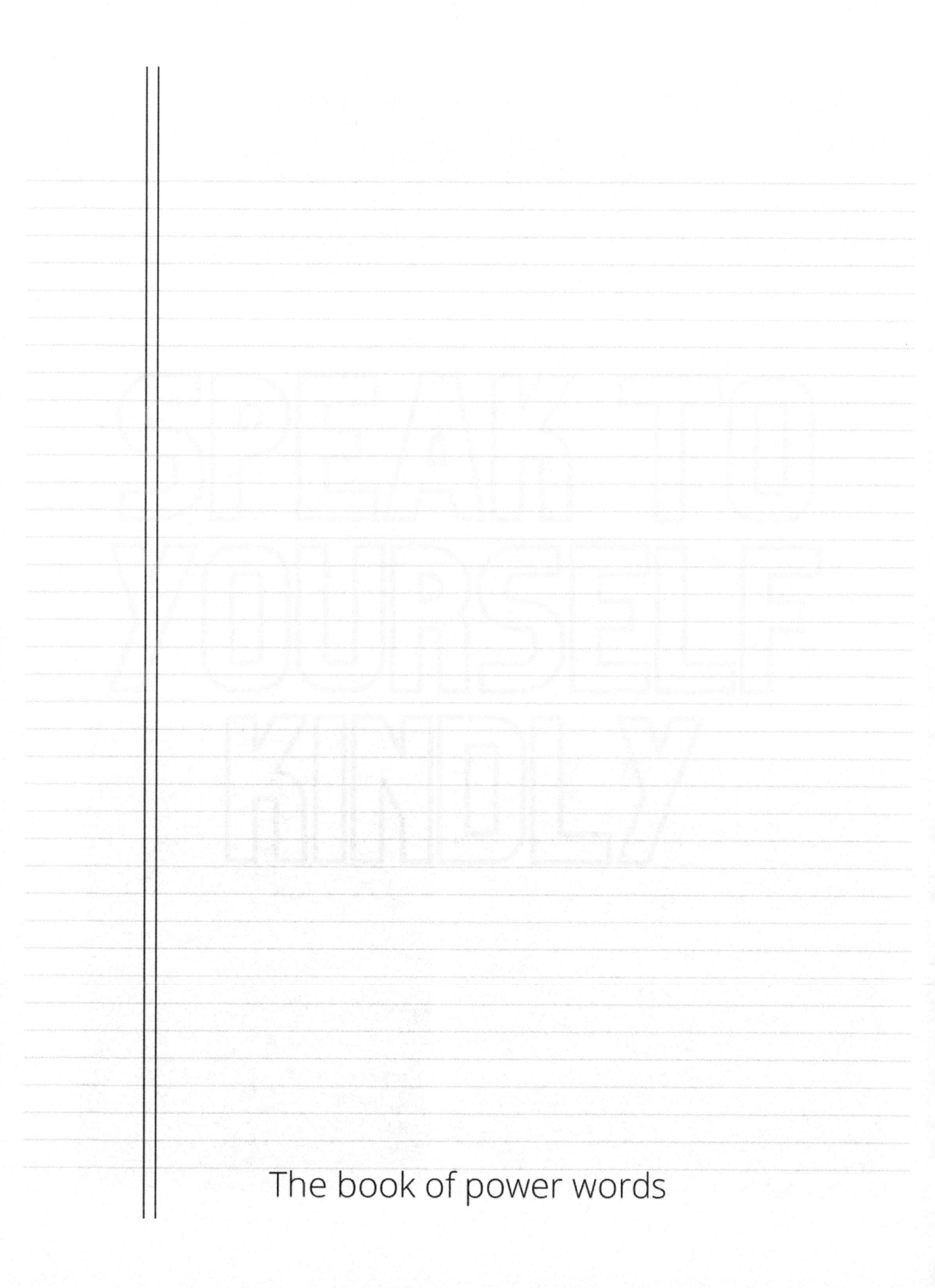

The book of power words

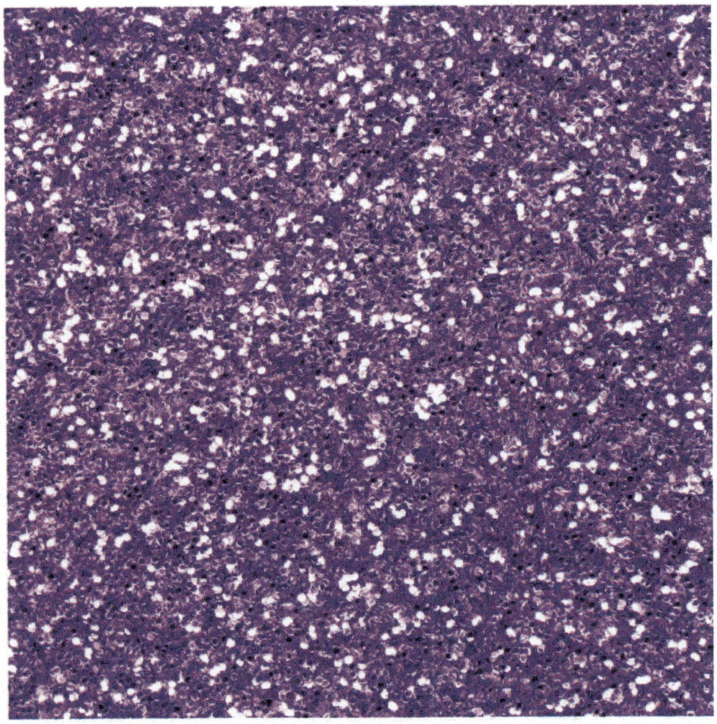

THOUGHTS BECOMES WORDS...

The book of power words.

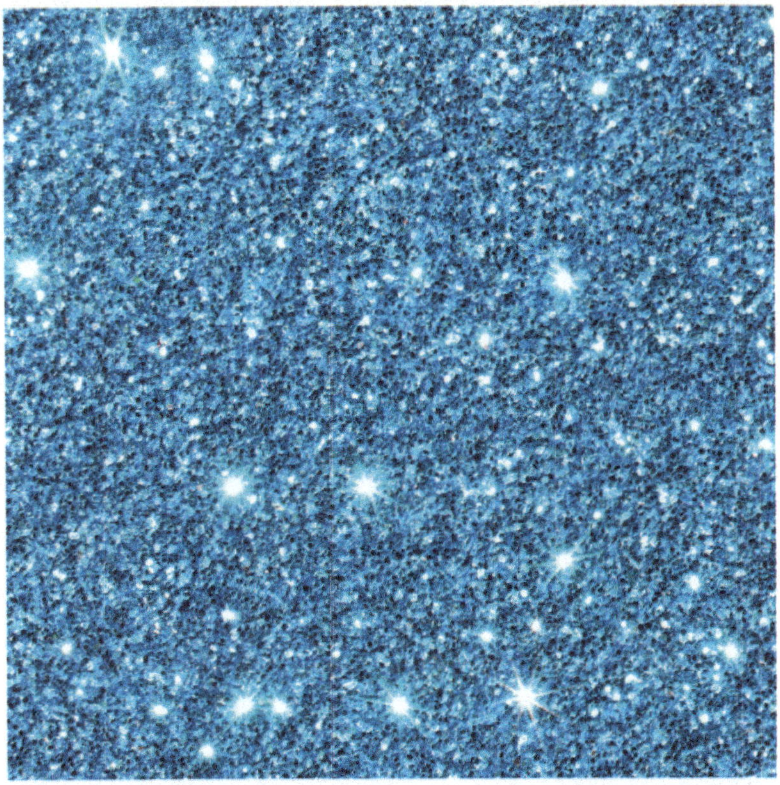

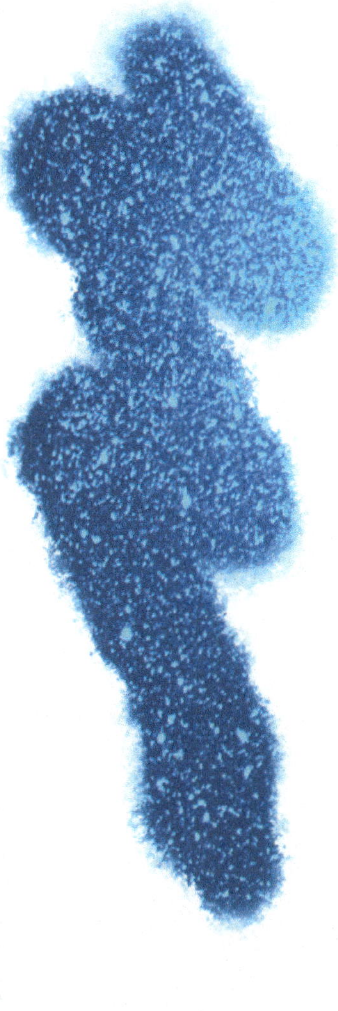
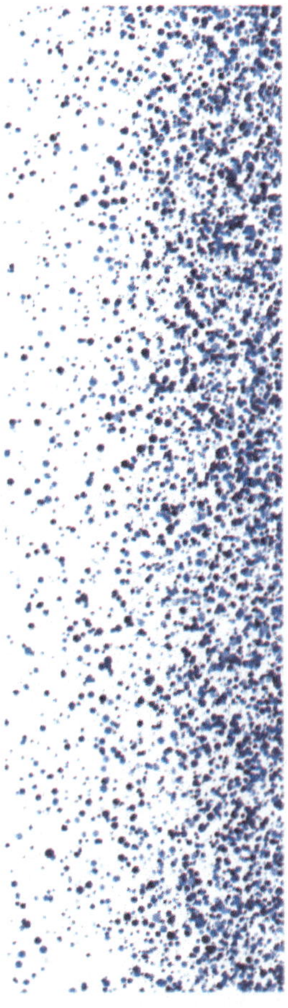

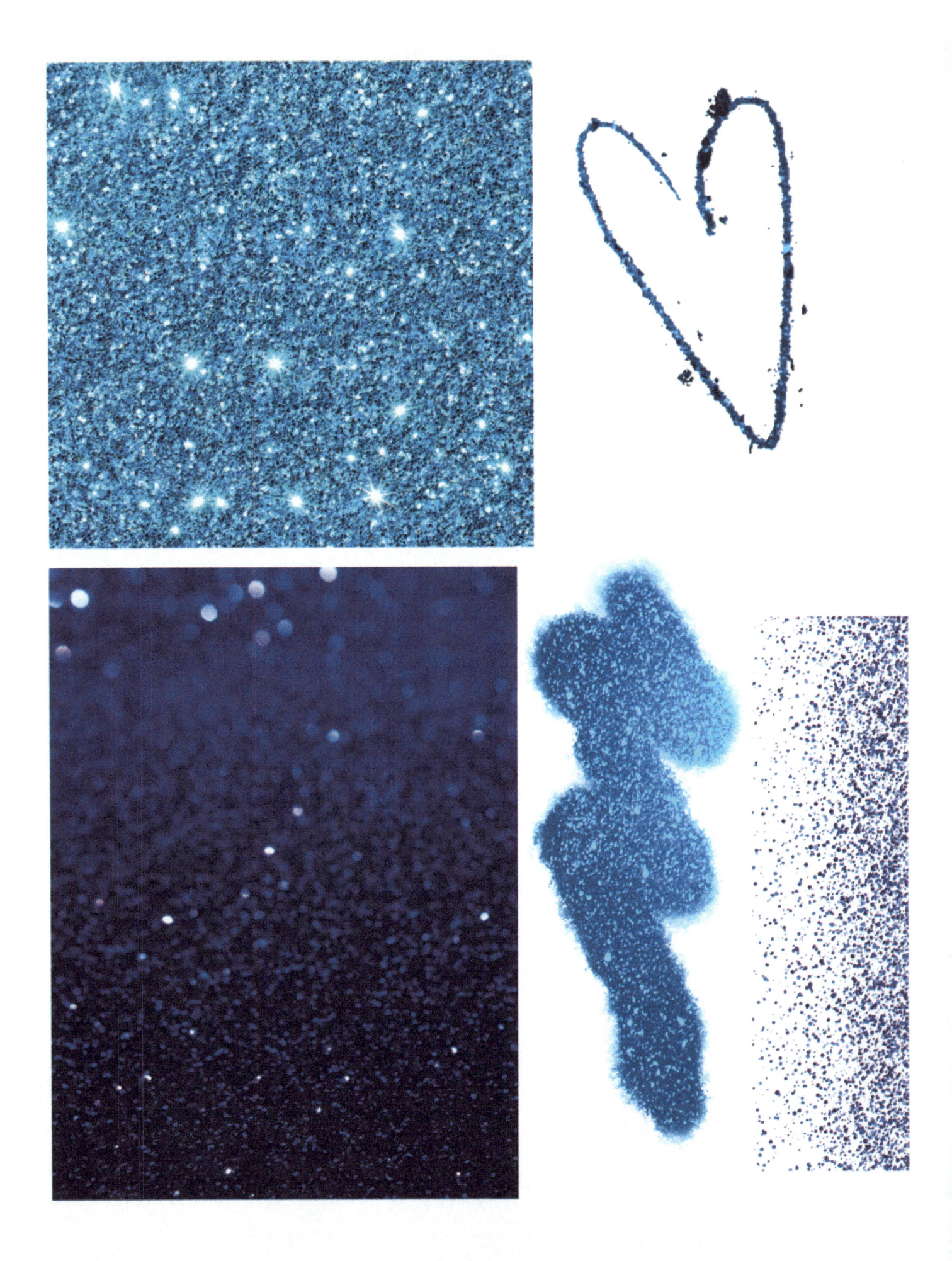

The book of power words

OPEN for
BUSINESS

FOR
SALE

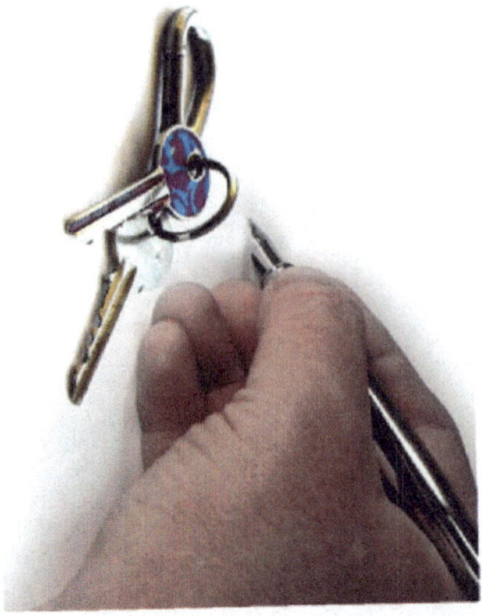

LIKE A BOSS

CONTRACT

Google

MAKE
MONEY

THOUGHTS BECOMES WORDS...

The book of power words.

Approved!

APPROVED

FOR RENT
FOR SALE
WELCOME HOME

CONTRACT

Assignment.
SIGNATURE

Marriage Certificate

APPROVED
APPROVED

THOUGHTS
BECOMES
WORDS...

The book of power words.

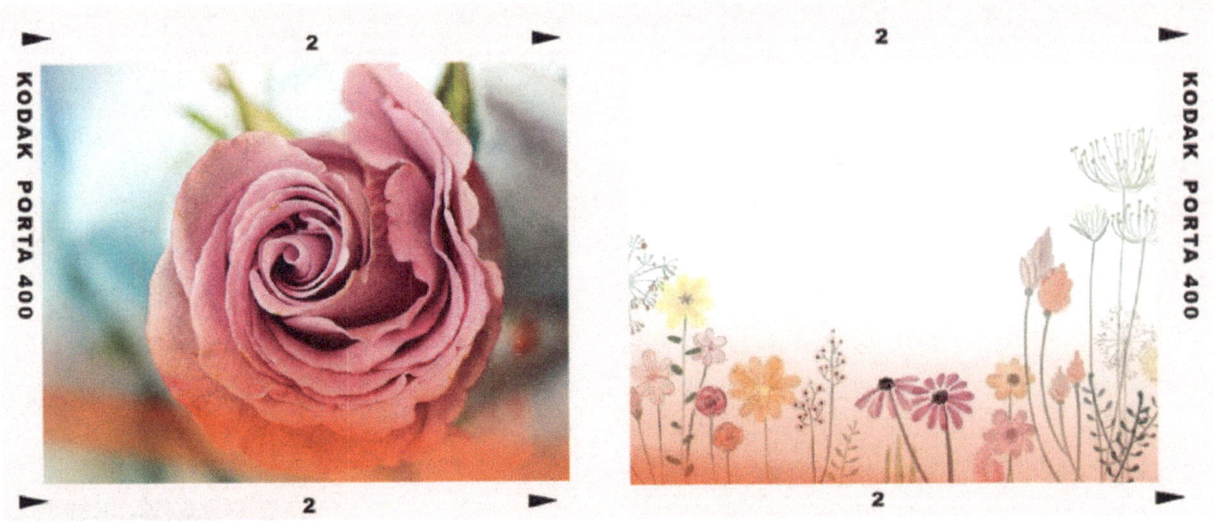
2
KODAK PORTA 400
2

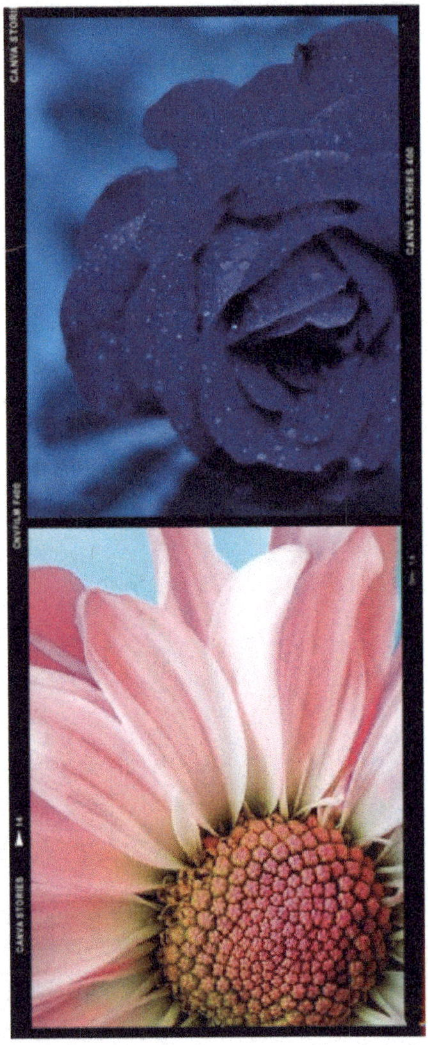
CANVA STORIES

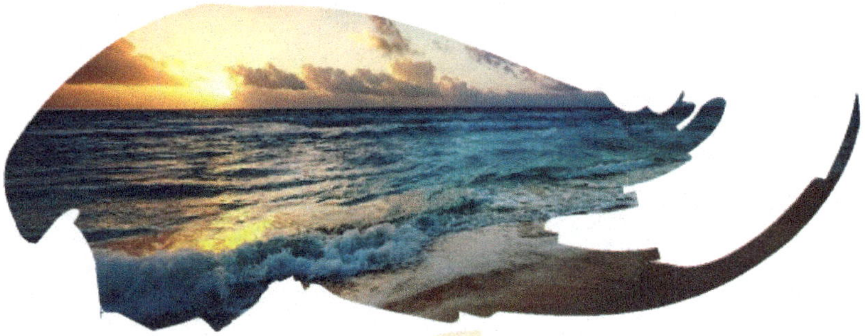

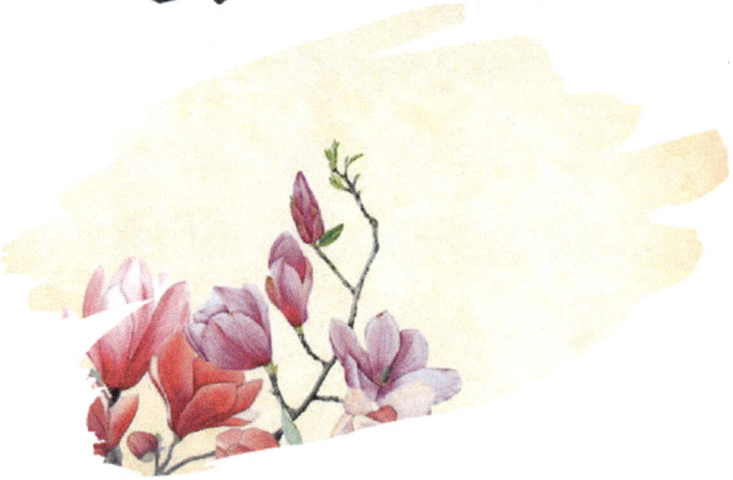

The book of power words

SPEAK TO YOURSELF KINDLY

The book of power words

A B C D E F
G H I J K L
M N O P Q R
S T U V W X
Y Z

THOUGHTS
BECOMES
WORDS...

The book of power words.

AABBCCDD
EEFFGGHHII
JJKKLLMM
NNOOPPQ
QRRSSTTU
UVVWWX
XYYZZ

SPEAK TO YOURSELF KINDLY

The book of power words

aabbccddeeff
gghhiijjkkllmm
nnooppqqrrssttuuvv
wwxxyyzz

aabbccddee
ffgghhiijjkk
llmmnnooppqqrrsstt
uuvvwwxxyyzz

The book of power words

AAA

BBB CCC

DDD EEE

FFF GGG

HHH III

JJJ KKK

The book of power words

LLLMMM
NNNOOOP
PPQQQRR
RSSSTTT
UUUVVV

SPEAK TO YOURSELF KINDLY

The book of power words

WWW

XXX

ZZZ

111122222

333444

The book of power words.

5556667
77
888999
0000

The book of power words.

WHAT YOU THINK, YOU CREATE.

What you imagine, you become.

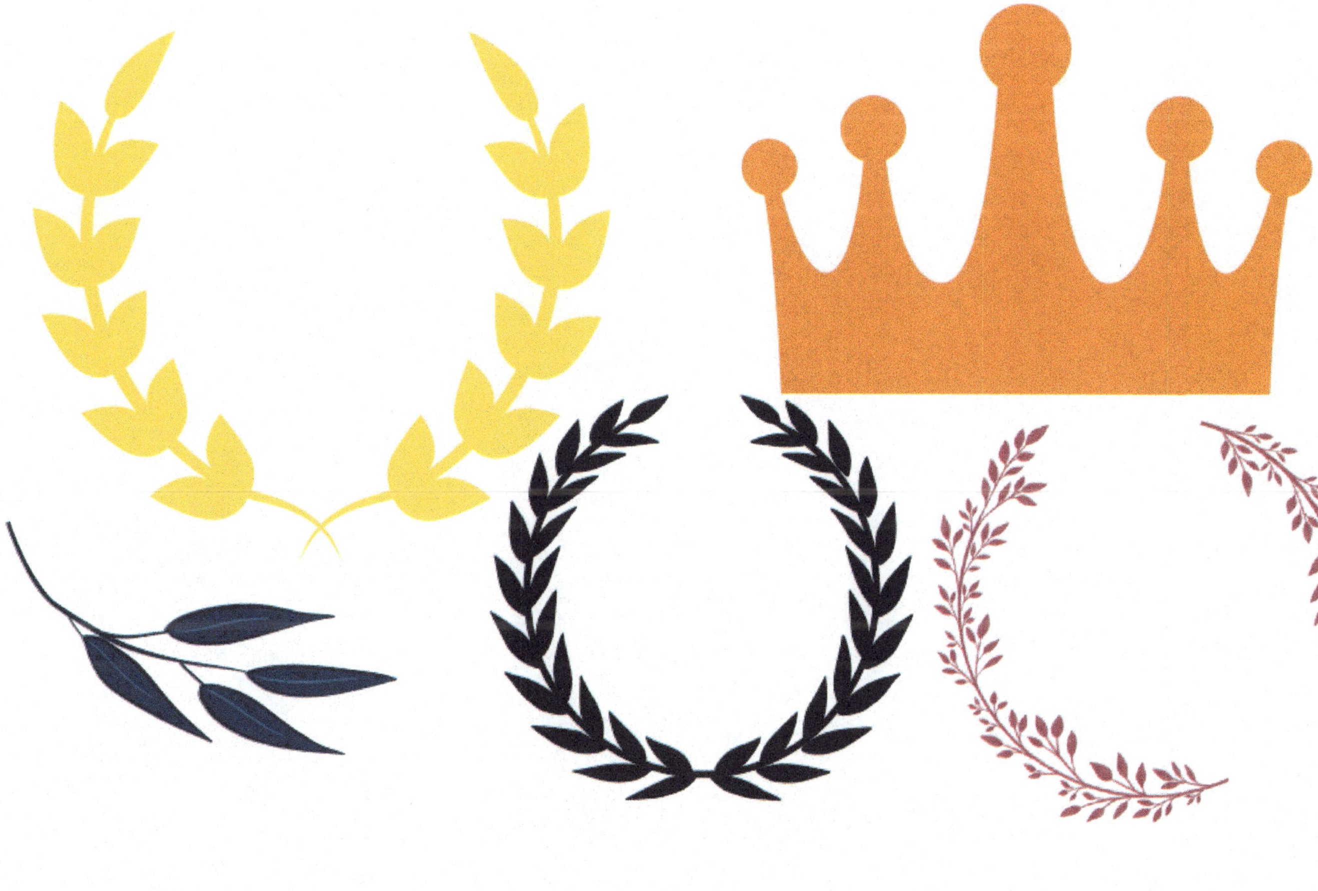

The book of power words

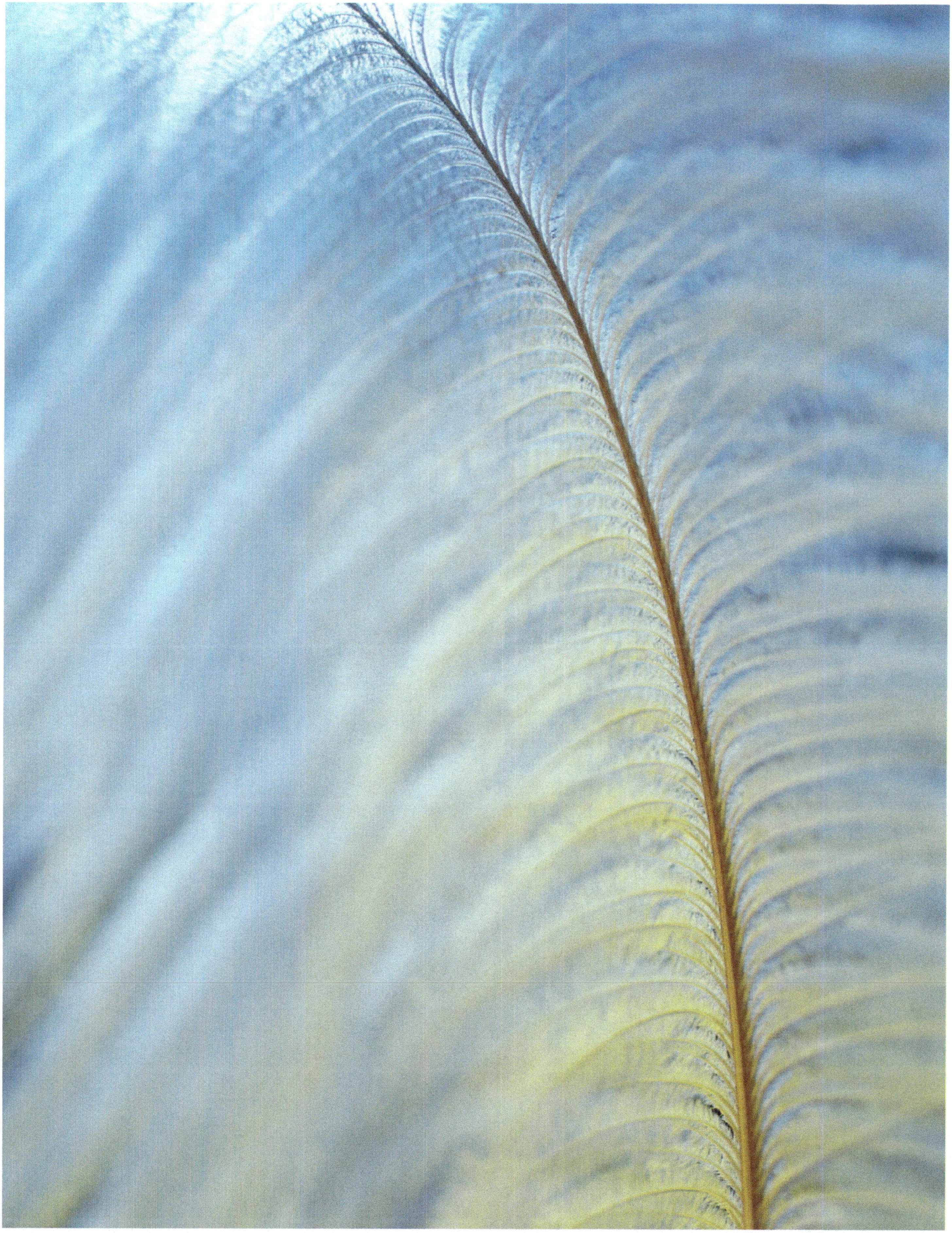

THOUGHTS BECOMES WORDS...

The book of power words.

THOUGHTS
BECOMES
WORDS...

The book of power words.

THOUGHTS
BECOMES
WORDS.

The book of power words.

THOUGHTS
BECOMES
WORDS...

The book of power words.

THOUGHTS
BECOMES
WORDS.

The book of power words.

THOUGHTS
BECOMES
WORDS.

The book of power words.

THOUGHTS BECOMES WORDS...

The book of power words.

THOUGHTS
BECOMES
WORDS.

The book of power words.

THOUGHTS BECOMES WORDS...

The book of power words.

THOUGHTS
BECOMES
WORDS.

The book of power words.

THOUGHTS
BECOMES
WORDS...

The book of power words.

THOUGHTS
BECOMES
WORDS...

The book of power words.

THOUGHTS BECOMES WORDS...

The book of power words.

THOUGHT
BECOMES
WORDS...

The book of power words.

THOUGHTS BECOMES WORDS.

The book of power words.

Made in the USA
Columbia, SC
21 September 2022

THOUGHTS BECOMES WORDS.

The book of power words.

The Book of POWER WORDS

AFFIRMATIONS/ CUT OUTS FOR VISION BOARD AND JOURNALS